Even More Words

- further reflections on Non-Duality

Graham Stew

For Lana

Prologue

There is nothing in this book for you. In fact, the message in these pages may be the death of you. Sounds hopeless? Good.
What follows is a mixture of words loosely addressing the theme of non-duality. They attempt to express the inexpressible, and because language is inevitably dualistic, they fail. The mind will never 'get' this message, so don't even try. Just let the words sink in without trying to think about what they mean. Something may happen - or not. Either way ... it's fine.

The story of our 'lives' is convincingly real. Emotions, thoughts and sensations arise constantly and are entertained and attended to – we believe the 'movie' is reality. The movie is all about 'me' … and guess who the star is …'ME'!

It is the ultimate deception … the cause of all problems and suffering. All inputs are related to a false 'self' and judged accordingly. Desire and aversion are experienced and we are caught in a continuous drama of wanting things to be other than they are.

But things are as they are … as they need to be … and are an invitation to understand what is real, and what is not. The very fact that experiences are fleeting and insubstantial should teach us that they are not real, and therefore we need not be attached to them. All thoughts, feelings and sensations are transient disturbances of energy … ripples across the surface of a lake … and are not who we really are.

What we really are is beyond all these phenomena; beyond concepts, words or thoughts. It is behind and 'upstream' of all ideas or mental activity, and to speak or write about this is impossible.

And yet … when suffering and illusion is witnessed, there arises the impulse to challenge ignorance, and to encourage inquiry, where possible. Each movie is different, however, and each journey must be completed in its own way. This message may not be heard, and should never be pushed. Those with ears to hear will hear the truth resonate inside the words.

The powerful illusion of time conditions us to believe that there is some future point when everything will be fine … enlightenment will occur … whatever. Enlightenment will not 'occur' to anyone … it IS. It is not an experience to be achieved, or a state to be gained. Experiences and states arise and pass away. THIS never changes.

Peace lies under all we are.
As the bedrock of mountains...
The springs of rivers...
The roots of trees...
So peace is our sure foundation.

We need nothing else;
But the mind invents desires,
Creates problems, and
Constructs our lives' stories ...
Unnecessary fictions.

The peace we seek
We already own.
If we cease searching
It will appear.
In the space between breaths
Is our true home and rest.

From the mind arise doubts,
Fears, depressions ...
But from what does the mind arise?
The answer is a deep, calm silence.

The cushion in my back,
the sound of Schumann,
and the August sunshine...
What more could there be?

Waiting in a classroom.
Silence and sunshine.
All the learning I need!

Empty classroom.
No knowledge ...
No problem!

When objects appear in consciousness
the universe is created;

Absence of any objects to be conscious of
is absolute peace.

We live not in time
but time lives in us.

We have invented past and future
through the action of thought.

All things arise in the present
which is this timeless moment.

When we live in a horizontal world,
thought create both memories and plans.

Lost in remembering and planning,
we lose touch with the peace of Now.

Writing the story of 'our lives' through
imagining an illusory identity,

We chase the mirage of future happiness,
and overlook the miracle of this moment.

Stop. Look. There is no suffering here,
free from the tyranny of the mind.

When does thinking have an end?
When does the intellect come to a halt?

Emptiness beckons …
peace is uncovered in the space between thought,
and there is a full stop to conception.

Perception continues …
Sensations arise within awareness;
Unconditioned, pre-verbal …
Too simple for words.

We can escape the self-obsession,
the endless rehearsal of our social presentation;
the cosseting of self-esteem.
Let it all blow away in the wind of realisation!

There is a moment when time stops
when the wind of change drops into silence;
the rush into the future is halted;
and stillness arises.

No thought can follow here …
no logic or understanding …
and so words fall away.

Just a silent 'knowing'
That all is perfection;
and that consciousness is all there is.

That we are safe,
because we are nothing.
That we can smile,
because we have everything.

So we move back into time …
letting all things take their course,
in the knowledge that All is Well.

———

How do we move from here to Here?
Keeping dry in the rain....
and sleeping without dreaming?
How can the eye see itself ...
or our teeth bite themselves?

Try breathing ...
Who is there to do that?
Life is breathing 'you' into existence.
The whole body-mind organism
is simply a movement of the universe.
An atom out of place ...
and the whole edifice would cease to be.

So we are nothing as individuals...
as entities we do not exist;
but as the Dance of Life
we are part and parcel of all there is.
No separation – just Joy!

Soaring birds, chasing down the wind,
flinging themselves into the naked energy
of a westerly gale.

An old tree has succumbed,
falling across the path,
forcing detours.

Hauling myself up the hill, against the wind,
I wondered if I too might succumb to its
insistent pushing.

Not today... but the time will come
when I will fall across others' lives,
causing detours ...
no more permanent than the wake of a
passing ship.

There is nothing here,
except a sequence of happenings.

Hearing seagulls;
feeling sun on the skin;
seeing these squiggles appear on paper,
noting the ideas which appear in awareness.

Nothing personal …
just Life unfolding as it must.
Must? … that implies purpose,
direction and meaning;
all concepts of the mind.

So, dropping the concepts,
all that remains is This …
the hum of the bees,
the warm embrace of a summer's day …
everything in its place
without the need for meaning.

Q. Is it difficult to be free?
A. Where are your chains?

But my mind gives me no peace!
Your mind has invented you.

How can I silence my mind?
Can your hand hold itself?

So I can do nothing?
Find the one who can do anything.

It all seems hopeless to me!
For the individual all is hopeless.

So life just happens?
All appears in awareness.

So this is all unreal?
If we believe a dream, then it seems real.

I will simply give up trying
Beware of trying to stop trying. Just Be.

Can we correct our first and fundamental mistake?

The fragmentation of unity ....

the error of ego ...

the meanness of 'me-ness'.

Can we regain the wonder of simply being here

in this eternal moment?

... not seeing through tired eyes

 and filtering reality through

cramped conditioning, personal prejudices

and social programming.

There is freedom now ...

Look!   All the atoms in the universe

are combining in this instant

to produce This ...

Is this not more than enough?

We weave the world into existence with our
thoughts.
Perceiving objects in consciousness,
we create our isolation.
What a dismal trick!

If we let thoughts arise and pass away;
lasting no longer than a breath,
then there is simply awareness of impermanence ....
an allowing of whatever
appears to simply be there;
a passing entertainment.

And what an entertainment!
Just watch in awe,
as life unfolds within Yourself.
Just as one dewdrop contains the world;
so one breath reveals
the wonder of being here.

The road to heaven starts and ends here.

Any move away from this

is a departure from reality.

Thinking is just a movement away from Now.

Allow what is here to be just the way it is …

saying 'Yes' to Life as it offers you

each amazing moment …

that is the only practice required.

Sit back and watch your life unfold;

you will react and respond according to your

conditioning and DNA programming.

It's never personal …

It's the universe whispering: "All is Well!"

The Way is not hard
If one learns to let go.

Let go of hope ... you will not gain liberation.
Let go of beliefs ... all concepts are meaningless.
Let go of identity ... you are not who
you think you are.
Sit back ... behind the appearances in the dream.
Watch the passing show of
thoughts and experiences.
Entertaining as they are... plausible and convincing;
yet essentially empty.
Relax into this emptiness ...
for it contains everything.

Warm September sunshine …

lengthening shadows and plants

that have given us pleasure

transform to winter colours of brown and black.

The tidying away of another summer.

Gratitude for what has been, and

hope for what may come…

next Spring, after the Winter storms.

Words are inadequate ...

there is just this endless stream of perception -

sunlight… warmth… breeze… noises.

This is more than enough!

What more is there to say?

The pen moves across the paper and words appear …

I don't know what they will be.

Do they mean anything?

Who is to say?

I can read the statement:

"There is no separation" …

and it can be interpreted in a narrow fashion;

or embraced as a symbol of insight and wisdom.

We can read: "All is One" …

but the intellectual understanding

nods in superficial agreement.

It doesn't hit home.

The truth has immense power

to destroy all beliefs and illusions,

and shine the light of awareness everywhere;

dispelling the darkness of ignorance.

What needs to be broken to allow the light in?

There is no 'thing' …

only false perception.

The old brain labelling and separating;

assessing and judging;

maintaining the defences of a fictitious self.

Where is the danger when all is One?

What is the threat when there is no 'other'?

No subject-object division;

only the immensity of All.

The streams and tributaries of thought

flow into the ocean of awareness;

where stillness and peace

are found … always and already!

The imagined story of a lonely self,

is seen through as a mirage,

and there is a coming home to This.

Whatever appears before you
cannot be you.
You are the one that watches
appearances come and go…
the mirror for all experiences;
and remains untouched and untouchable.

All that is perceived is transient,
insubstantial as clouds,
and as fleeting as lightning
in a summer sky.

Why then would we attach
any importance to these things?
They are not us; we did not
produce them, or choose them.

Sit back, relax, and enjoy the show.
There's no entrance fee,
and you can leave whenever you wish!

Energy is in all things
…. IS all things.
Within this energy there is no separation,
although it expresses itself
in countless ways.

In this way all things
share the same nature …
and all division is artificial.
The energy within thoughts
can coalesce into beliefs,
causing mental stagnation.

Leaving thoughts alone…
letting them flow,
is freedom in action.
Watching sensations appear
and float away like clouds is liberation.
Allow energy to destroy your prison walls
by simply letting it be.

Despite the nagging chatter
of the mind,
things are accomplished.

Despite the judgment and criticism
of our prejudices,
All is well.

Despite all beliefs and dogmas,
the Truth silently invites
our awareness.

Reality is waiting in stillness
to be recognised, and
remembered as our birthright.

No great achievement,
this movement in all it is simplicity
is all we ever need.

No movement away from what is here;
no waiting for future change …
so maddeningly obvious!

———

What if all the world screams: "WHY?!"
... would there be an answer?
Could there be an explanation of this
mystery
... of all this pain, separation and misery
... of all this wonder, joy and beauty?

No ... no answers from the mind
will ever suffice.
No theories from earnest priests
or confident scientists
will do.

Dropping all beliefs...
letting go all attempts at an answer ...
a silent smile ...
and perhaps a flower in the hand?

Very little motivation to write..

so why do I lift the pen?

All the words have been written

by others more eloquent than I.

Any more concepts simply add

to the overloaded mind,

and offer further confusion.

The answer to all questions

lies in silence …

a quiet knowing,

letting go of all beliefs, hopes and ideals.

Everything must be dropped …

even the concept of someone dropping everything.

All must go …

then, empty of form,

the formless may appear.

Only Awareness -
and that which appears within it.
Consciousness in three forms -
dependent on the Ground of Being.
All objects appearing in consciousness –
thoughts, feelings, perceptions.

Any movement, change or impulse –
just another appearance.
We are all appearances -
everything we know,
remember or imagine.
And we are That to which we appear …
Absolute Oneness.

The pen awaits its instruction …
and the intellect must be put to one side.
The mind must get out of the way.

Then, perhaps … from the silence;
meaning may arise
and words form on the page.

Sometimes the message flows,
unimpeded by thought,
and something like Truth
flickers into life.

At other times there is the
critical judgment of the mind …
comparing and evaluating,
neutering the fertile.

Letting go is the secret;
letting be all that breathes
and moves through our days…
regarding nothing as important.

Who were you before
you were given an identity?
Isn't it worth going back there
to find out?

Don't hope or believe …
they take you away from
the truth of what is.

The journey home begins
and ends here…
So don't pack for this trip.
You won't need anything.

You can leave behind
all concepts, theories,
dogmas and teachings.

Be empty … as you truly are …
Capacity for all things …
even your false identity!

Which dream do we wake up from?
Each morning a new start …
stepping into the costume;
assuming the customary role.

We have played this part of 'me'
so much that we don't need
to think about it.
Like an old coat,
it hangs comfortably on us.

That's where the illusion begins.
The 'coat' is not who we are …
it is a parcel of assumptions
in the melodrama we call 'our life'.

Without the coat, the role,
the memories, opinions and
'knowledge' that fill our brains;
what are we?
The answer is waiting in silence
for the dreaming to end.

Consciousness enjoys being …
and so everything arises
in this conscious presence.
… and flows, like an unending river
that loves its journey over rocks
and through obstacles …
always changing and always the same.
Just water shaping itself
in cosmic entertainment.

We are this water … this cascade
of sentient bubbles that rushes
forward from moment to moment;
exulting in the energy;
moving through ripples,
waves, eddies and whirlpools.

Can you see what you really are?
The senses, thoughts and emotions
that Consciousness creates
for Its own enjoyment.

Sitting quietly
watching the breath.
Autumn comes ...
and the leaves fall by themselves.

———————◦———————

The snow-globe of the mind settles;

the muddy water clears ...

and we find ourselves where we always were.

Free of concepts, reality is easier to see.

It's just 'what is' ...

this unfolding pattern of energy which moves

every sub-atomic particle in the universe

-      or appears to.

For behind all the appearances

the silent emptiness is all there isn't!

———————◦———————

Like so many falling leaves,
wisdom is easily blown away
by the youthful wind of change.

Lessons learned in the cauldron
of Life's hardships
are swept into oblivion.

Unshared, unrecognised ...
the chance to imbibe
insights from elders is lost.

Perhaps each of us has to
face the challenge of experience alone?
Making sense anew?

So the world turns toward winter;
spurning the light of growth
and resigned to approaching darkness.

Spring seems far away ...
the cold seeps deeper into the soul ...
but Life knows the light will return.

How to find your way Home?
Find out what's stopping you ...
and then drop it!

What is preventing you from
seeing/knowing who you really are,
is a phantom ... an illusion.

The story of 'me'... so carefully
composed and conditioned
over the imagined years.
The hard shell of the ego,
which appears to separate us from the
world,
is paper thin!
It can be seen through,
just like a dream upon waking.

What an extraordinary and amazing experience …
simply being alive!
Surely there must be a purpose
to this consciousness … this being here?
If not, then what a glorious accident!

Scarlet viburnum leaves …

what beauty in

growing old!

The Seven A's

We begin *in* and *as* Awareness, and sensations and
thoughts appear;
objects to which we may Attend;
recognising their presence, we Acknowledge them;
interpreting their meaning we Allow
them to simply be here ….
Accepting that this is how things are right now …
Appreciating the richness of experience,
and bidding Adieu to all things as they pass away,
returning to the empty fullness of Awareness.

Have you ever been lost in a film or a book? Absorbed in the story, identifying with the characters? They seem so real that you share their joys and sorrows as if they were your own. The experience is so vivid and powerful that it becomes your reality. The thoughts, feelings, hopes, fears and actual sensations are perceived as 'mine'. The drama becomes 'my life' … and what a show it is!

The triumphs and tragedies; joys and sorrows; laughter and tears … all so gripping and apparently real. Since the age of two we have regarded 'our lives' as individual journeys through a harsh and uncaring world. Needing to protect our vulnerable selves from whatever the world throws at us. What a stupid and sorry mistake!

The Cosmic Joke

The eye that sees you
is the eye that sees me.
In truth, there is no separation.
The only division is in the mind,
which discriminates and judges.

There is movement, of course,
which is perceived by logic in terms of cause and
effect.
But there are no causes or effects.
Everything moves together.
All things are inter-connected and inter-dependent.

So my belly rises with the breath
that the Universe is moving into me;
just as the trees outside
are swaying with the same air!

Broken fence ...
the wind will enjoy
waving it.

Today is Remembrance Day ...
We are supposed to remember those who were killed in wars.
This is a story we choose to believe.
Our world is littered with stories.
Stories make up our lives,
that is - our lives are made up of fictions.

We live - a product of imagination.
Some stories are forgotten;
others recalled in detail ...
Some matter more than others.
Some are questioned ... most believed.

Stepping away from stories into this new moment,
the mind falls silent,
unable to label or judge ...
there is just the falling rose petal ...
the falling notes of music.

God is dancing with Herself …
            inventing partners to embrace
                        and with whom to move through Life.

These imaginary dancers are ourselves …
            deluded, we believe we choose our steps.

We don't know this dance …
            the moves are strangely familiar,
                        but not of our choice
                                    and out of our control.

We think it will end soon,
            but there was no beginning;
                        only a perpetual motion
                                    of arising and passing away.

The dancers are God and our 'selves' …
            pretending separation;
                        where there is only One …
                                    loving to move.

Letting

Letting in the Sacred,
turning from the word
to the Spirit that lives.

That lives and waits in the silence
that rests beneath
the turmoil of thought.

Always here … complete and perfect;
watching the seeking in the wrong place -
the pursuit of delusions and dreams.

Always home … ready to welcome
the wandering soul's return
from its fruitless search.

Seeing with new insight,
beyond the mind's complications,
to the simplicity of Letting Be …
accepting all with love and joy …
and then Letting GO!

How many times has it been said?
 How many more times must it be said?
 There is no 'Other'!
This is it! ... in its entirety.
This whole marvellous, awful mess
of a world that we call home.

This projection/appearance in our awareness
... not yours or mine.
This knowing of Itself ...
 this Self-Consciousness.
Until this is known,
 the pantomime of separation continues –
ripping apart Oneness into
ridiculous little 'egos' ...
a sad and meaningless farce.

Statements

This is appearing in Consciousness.

Consciousness contains all things

and all things are expressions of Consciousness.

Consciousness is not a thing,

 but gives birth to all things.

As all objects appear and disappear

they are not real but relative.

They are conditional.

Underneath all appearances is

Peace – Silence – Perfect Rest.

We are already there!

Nothing to achieve.

Nothing to gain.

Nowhere to go.

Just relax into Being!

The Lake

A silent lake whose surface is a smooth mirror.
Such is the still mind,
the mind unsullied by thought.

Let the breeze of cognition move, and there are ripples
…
appearing and subsiding again into glassy reflection.

The lake reflects everything, but needs nothing …
contains and accepts all, but is not touched by anything.

Storms arise - great boulders can crash into the lake
and cause huge waves, tumult and disturbance.

Do nothing – keep watching, and the water will
resume its glassy stillness of peace.
Such is the contemplative state.

**Sick of words,
I listen to the wind
speak instead.**

Like follows dislike … follows like…
and so the day passes.

Knowing the liking/disliking
neutralises experience …
the watching provides sanctuary …
and the muddy water slowly clears.

Acknowledging; Allowing; Accepting;
these three A's are the answer.

Why wage war on reality?
Just this is all we need …
more than we need.
The riches are overwhelming.

The taste of melon; the sound of Miles Davis;
cushions in my back; smell of freshly-made coffee;
this Saturday morning …
This amazing show … a slice of JOY!

How much Being is there in this
wet and windy day?
No more, no less than any other ...
Life is always already
complete in presenting experience.

The mind wanders ... and wonders
what more should be ... surely this is not enough -
this sitting and watching the restless mind.

Something to show for the day?
Wasting time seems to be a crime.
I have nothing to show.
... another day nearer death in the
calendar of this 'life'.
What does that mean?
The rational mind sees a finite lifetime ebbing away ...
the body and mind remorselessly ageing;
... but this humming aliveness speaks of eternity.

Awareness is all there is … in moving
it produces objects of consciousness
which create our world.

The objects include the sense of 'us'.
Observing these objects thus creates
the division between subject and object.

There is only perceiving …
no separation into perceiver and perceived.
This fundamental error is the source of
alienation from Being.

It is only the mind that makes distinctions;
and thus creates this isolated individual,
who senses that something of value has been lost.

It is not lost …
it is always here …
closer than this breath!

DECEMBER

There's nothing personal in this ...
watching thoughts and emotions
float by in spacious awareness.

This moment contains the universe
and both time and space
contract within this breath.

Weather and winter and the
butt-end of another year
blow through this openness.

And as full as the mind is ...
in its nagging dissatisfactions,
there is always, already, peace.

The peace that lies beneath
the heartache of a flooded home
or the pain of loss.

Beneath the agonies and disasters,
the year turns towards 2017
in a quiet and natural serenity.

We must remember the relative
and not confuse it with the Absolute.

Identifying with the mind and body
requires consideration of safety,
food, income, social needs, etc.

That becomes the story of 'our lives',
and any contact or knowledge
of any deeper consciousness is lost.

We fall asleep in the melodrama
and suffer as a result ...
Our sleep becomes a nightmare.

We fear death, yet we also fear
the experiences of loss and desire
that life offers us.

All that is experienced is a lesson ...
an opportunity to learn that we are
so much more than we imagine;
and yet not even that!

Just sitting is enough –
just this breath;
this moving of air ... of thought ... of sensations.

Sounds arriving at the door of consciousness;
unbidden but accepted.
Hearing happening without listening ...
allowing and acknowledging all.

Choosing, preferring, judging, rejecting;
all these are absent in this
open, choiceless awareness.
All is as it should be ... as it is.

Who or why on earth would we
want anything to be other than it is?
What madness to declare that **This**
is somehow insufficient or wrong!

Outside the mind, there is no time.
Not even eternity - not even an endless now.
Beyond the concepts of past, present and future …
just This.
And yet … our little selves live in time
and are situated somewhere.
The charade unfolds, and the mind
creates the story of 'me' and my life.

The performance can continue, by all means,
but here the mask has slipped;
the play is revealed as this constructed tragi-comedy;
and although entertaining, remains
essentially false and meaningless.
Letting it be, and relaxing into the real Me…
I enjoy the show!

**Washing –
Dressing –
Eating –
Who is doing all these?**

Prose Pointers

We are Awareness. Sometimes referred to as Consciousness, Presence, Spirit, Absolute, the Self, the Unborn, or our Natural State. The capitalisation indicates that what we are is 'special'. Awareness is simply that which perceives. It perceives sensations through the five senses; and thoughts and feelings through the mind (the sixth sense). Through perception, the world, body and mind appear. Perception requires consciousness . Without consciousness... no perception... and no existence.

Spiritual seekers and philosophers tend to complicate matters. They believe that 'Awareness' is something to be sought and achieved. Something to be gained after strenuous effort and practice. This is not true.

Awareness is here now; closer than the nose on our face. We are like those people who search for the glasses which are perched on the top of their head. Without awareness there would be no perception - no objects; no world; no us. It allows us to experience all phenomena. Are you aware right now? Of course you are ... if you are reading these words; and are conscious of your body and the thoughts seeking to make sense of this message.

You are aware of your existence ... you know that you *are*. There's no doubt about that, is there? You are conscious of being aware ... after all, we are *homo sapiens sapiens* ... the only creature that knows ... and knows that it knows. So there you have it - you are

Awareness … consciousness being aware of itself. Simple? Yes, but also immensely profound.

Phenomena. What are these objects that appear in awareness? … and who or what is perceiving them? Is there a perceiving subject and an object that is perceived? Or is there just 'perceiving'? As J. Krishnamurti stated: *"The observer is the observed"*. In the phenomenal world there are separate objects to be perceived by a subject. Noumenally there is only awareness without objects. No separation … just One without a second.

Phenomena are things, appearances, mental events which are observable. Attending to these appearances 'outside' the world is created through our senses. Shifting attention 'inside' creates awareness of 'the body'. Directing attention to thoughts and feelings, the 'mind' is created. Before, between and beyond these phenomena is Noumenon; that which cannot be described because it has no qualities. Outside time and space, it contains all appearances but is unchanged by them. All phenomena arise and pass away, but the Noumenon is always present as capacity for everything. It is not even eternal, as it is timeless. Because whatever is real never changes, it is Reality.

Movements of consciousness create phenomena. Just as a still lake is disturbed by a single ripple, so does consciousness disturb the peace of the Absolute. Consciousness at rest is noumenal awareness. The world is perceived through the physical senses, and creates the illusion that the 'subject' is limited and separate. Exploring consciousness we sense that our awareness is infinite and without boundaries. This intuitive knowledge drives the search to discover who we really are. This sense of 'something missing' provokes the investigation to find out if there is something beyond the materialism of subject/object duality.

Awareness seeks to be aware of Itself; consciousness enjoys its own show!

In the mind, all perceptions are constantly changing … all experiences are impermanent. Yet conscious awareness remains unchanged throughout. Observation of phenomena demonstrates that consciousness never changes. The awareness that experienced our 'selves' as a five year old child, a fifteen year old teenager, and then a fifty year old, has always been the same. As Francis Lucille states: *"Consciousness of change is evidence of the changelessness of consciousness".*

This is good news. We are the awareness of objects that appear and disappear. We are the Subject that is conscious of transient objects. If we can observe objects come and go, we cannot **be** them. What we are is therefore outside of time, space and form; and is unchanging. Paradoxically, we are perceivers of objects and are simultaneously the objects that are perceived. We are the container and its contents … the awareness and the appearances. As witnessing awareness, we can either identify with these appearances, or remain free and limitless. Most identify with the body and mind, and this preserves a sense of separation. Such division is the source of all suffering.

Only awareness has freedom ... and that is our natural state ... our birthright. It requires no effort to let go of our mistaken beliefs, and to see through illusions. Reality is available always; already perfect ... waiting to be seen. Glimpses of reality can build to a clear certainty ... a safe knowing of what is real and what is false. Problems are seen through as products of the mind ... actions are taken as needed, but there is no associated suffering. If there is no desire for anything to be other than it is, then no suffering arises. Nothing is 'minded', and we live in the Grace of knowing who we truly are.

We are not other than Everything. Nothing exists apart from us ... we contain all things. We are the Ocean of Life on which all waves play ... the limitless Sky in which all types of weather come and go. Only habits of mind, persistent beliefs and our conditioning prevent us from realising the truth. Dropping these burdens, can we reach a state of 'not-knowing'? Can we open up to the moment-by-moment lessons that Life is offering? Every experience is an opportunity to see the truth of impermanence, and to drop the delusion of separation.

In the infinite space of awareness, all things appear. Thoughts, feelings, memories, ideas, images ... all arise and pass away. Since we can observe these appearances that arise within us, they cannot be us. All phenomena come and go, and as we observe them, we realise that they are not what we are. They are merely temporary objects appearing on the screen of awareness ... which

is our true identity. We do not create our thoughts ....
we have no clue as to what our next thought might be.
Neither are we the doer of our deeds ... actions
certainly occur, but where is the actor?

Things appear to happen, and through the mechanism
of the body/mind we can be aware of these objects.
Seeing their true nature, which is transient and
inherently unreal, there is a realisation that nothing
exists independently of the perceiving. There must be
perception for anything to appear in consciousness.
Without conscious awareness nothing can exist. We
come to see that what we called the world and 'our
lives' was a dream state ... a movie projected onto the
screen of awareness, and mistaken as being real.

Who Am I?

Thus, if we are not the actors of our actions, or the
thinkers of our thoughts ... who are we? To whom do
these thoughts arise?

Investigating this question erodes the ego; the sense of
self that has been constructed over the years, and whose
energies are spent in desperate self-preservation.
Discover that there is no place from which thoughts
arise, or to which they appear, and the story of self is
seen as the illusion it is. For the mind/body ... there is
'nobody home'! The mind as a collection of thoughts
is contained within awareness, and naturally cannot
perceive anything greater than itself. Being part of a
whole, it cannot comprehend that from which it was
born. When it realises that it is beyond its ability to

know its true nature, the mind stops, and in that silence Truth can be seen. Mental activity drops away, and awareness is simply conscious of itself. Our natural state as love, happiness and limitless awareness is revealed. Now there is so much space that the cramped meanness of judging good or bad can no longer function.

This does not mean that the mind must be ignored, suppressed or avoided. The mind can gain 'relative' knowledge of the truth, and can lead us to the threshold of insight. Then the mind must be transcended and left behind. If we use a boat to cross a river, we do not need to pick it up and carry it thereafter. Just as we can use a thorn to remove another thorn, and then throw both away, so we can use the mind as a tool to unlock the prison of the little self ... but Grace is needed for the step outside into freedom. Only then is it discovered that there never was a prison, and nothing to be liberated from. Another analogy is the stick we might use to stir the fire ... once it has served its purpose it is burned in the flames. Such is the mind.

If we believe we are individuals then the greatest curse is invited ... that of separation. All the world's troubles, throughout history, are the direct result of separation ... between people, religions, race or nationality. But this belief in being a separate self is only a thought; albeit a persistent and powerful one. This thought appears in awareness, like all other thoughts, and can be observed arising and passing away. It is not real, nor is it a fact. Letting go of this illusion; all that remains is open choiceless awareness

… just This … Oneness. The truth is that there is no duality … the distinction between subject and object is the work of the mind. All that is required to see this is quiet, patient observation. A simple inquiry into what is Real.

All objects arise in consciousness - and are part of consciousness; thus there is no duality in Truth.

Our belief in a separate self is just that - a belief, which is another thought. But the ego (a mental construction) protects this belief desperately … without it the individual would cease to exist. As the witnessing awareness, we can see how the mind labels and divides: this is me … that is not… separating life into self and other. We observe our body and thus cannot be it. We observe our thoughts and feelings, and so logically, cannot be them either. In fact, there is no one observing, just observation happening. Let me repeat this …. no observer … simply observing.

The conclusion is that everything we have previously identified with … mind, body and the world, is not what we really are. With that realisation comes a true sense of freedom … a putting down of a burden which has been carried for many years. This liberation has been here always - it is not new.

We have already been free, but we were unaware of our true state, because of conditioning and our mind's actions of discriminating, labelling and judging. There was nowhere we needed to go; nothing we needed to achieve. Just waking up to what is already here … in plain sight … an open secret.

We are conscious awareness - not confined within a body - in fact not located anywhere. We are infinite and outside of time and space. The mind has to fall silent, as this cannot be known or understood intellectually. The presence that we are is universal and impersonal, and all experience arises and dissolves in this Beingness. All that does appear is the same substance as Awareness ... the world of objects and people ... all are inherently consciousness. There is truly no separation ... no duality. But rather than accepting this statement intellectually, investigation is needed for the mind to discover its own non-existence. Logic can be used to destroy itself, but of course, there is no-one to do this!

The secret?
Not to mind anything!

January sunshine
Early daffodils
Puzzled frogs

What cannot be known must be lived;
What cannot be understood must be loved.

The mind has created duality through labelling the world as separate from you. Seeing life dualistically means dividing everything into contrasting opposites: up/down; in/out; good/bad; you/me; etc. The limited and conditioned mind is the result of consciousness forgetting its true identity, and falling into this human dream. What follows is an apparent sequence of experiences and perceptions of objects. We take this world of duality as a true representation of reality.

There is a knowing through the senses – here we can perceive the world as it appears to exist 'outside'.

Then there is a knowing through the mind – here we can observe thoughts and feelings come and go 'inside'.

But **what** is knowing these things?

This is the third way of knowing … a silent, pre-verbal, non-conceptual awareness. It does not move; it has no characteristics; it cannot be sensed or understood rationally. Yet it is always present.

It is consciousness without an object. Empty, yet capacity for all.

Not a thing, but containing all things … and **THAT** is what we truly are!

Ants nest —
who gives the orders?

Look to see who is thinking ...
            are you doing the thinking?
Are you working your breath ...
            or is breathing just happening?
Look to see if there is a personal cause of any
phenomena appearing in awareness.
Isn't everything simply arising and
passing through consciousness?
Spontaneously ... causelessly ... perfectly.

Yet the mind labels, judges, claims responsibility and
then wishes for things to be different. Never satisfied ...
it's nothing more than a critical and grumpy bag of old
mental habits.
Drop the bag ... it will continue chattering; but pay
attention to the space that surrounds all perceptions.
That silence is singing within your Heart!

This message does not bring any hope – in fact it destroys all hope - all belief.
This message is not for any individual …
it is the death of all persons.
If you can face the death of self; the loss of all hope; the end of all beliefs …
and see the emptiness of all things;
then who you truly are may finally be known.
The game will be over … the mirage seen through … the cosmic joke enjoyed.
And a smile as big as the universe
may spread across your original face!

Thoughts are simply ripples on the surface of the mind.
Sit quietly, watching … and they will settle into silence.
In that way, consciousness moves towards Awareness;
duality become non-dual.
Separation can be experienced
as an exchange between an imaginary subject and a supposed object.
The world, the body, and all perceptions appear in this consciousness.
Enjoy the show … marvel at this creation …
but do not be fooled into believing there is anything Real here.
Identification with the false leads only to suffering…
letting go into the Real is true freedom.

Older Now

A silent love holds all in place,
guarding the doors of the senses
against the marauding sorrows...
the pains of existence.

The cost of being seems too high at times;
the effort to keep engaged ...
needing wits and eyes open ...
too much altogether.

And still the silent love waits and watches;
not anywhere and in no time.
Just here ... behind the little story of a life.

A life being lived, by no-one ...
spontaneous, unplanned, empty ...
essentially meaningless.

The puppet man moves more slowly now,
sensing some denouement ...
falling into silent Love.

A few more aphorisms

You need a personality to function in the world; but it cannot define who you are.

Who you think you are does not even come close to who you really are.

Look behind the stories; beyond the concepts. There freedom, beauty and love are to be found.

Any 'person' looking for peace will never find it.

Everything is being taken care of – relax!

The light of our natural state has been eclipsed by the shadow of an illusory self.
This 'entity' is extended in time and space, and once it has completed its journey,
the light returns, having always been shining.

You are 'being lived' … it's not personal - so sit back and enjoy the ride!

You don't own your thoughts …
they come and go as they please.
How can they be owned? Where is there any owner?

What you are searching for is to be found in the place where the search starts.
Where are you looking from?

That's where you will find freedom.

How wonderful that nothing lasts for ever!

We can love every precious moment …
even the passing away of all perceptions.

Your natural state is available right now … just here …
don't look elsewhere. Just let it all settle.

Not swimming … just waving …
letting the currents of Life carry us
on our unique journey
– all Being is Becoming.

True happiness is a reflection of our innate nature.
Why look elsewhere for it?

Strive to be no-one … but remember there is no-one to
do any striving!

Any real happiness that you experience derives from
your original nature.

Let all things take care of themselves.

There is no cause of happiness,
as it is your natural state of being .

The bad news is that you are falling -
the good news is that there is no bottom!

The world is one huge entertainment; but don't seek
happiness there – it lies within.

Before the next thought arrives – rest there.

Nothing needs to be fixed, to be improved, to be a
certain way.
Everything is just fine as it is.
Just stop. Rest within.

If you don't like the way things are, you are inviting
suffering to come and live with you.

What is happening now does not involve a future.
Pay attention to just this – now.

The mind does what it needs to – your identification
with its games is optional.

Thoughts create emotions, which are felt in the body.
Attending to them simply feeds the feelings.
You can end fear, anger, depression – all of them –
by shifting attention to that which never changes.

You have had enough of these troubles … let them go
and embrace peace.

Do not search for what you already are …
that is wasting energy.
Be still and silent – realise that you are free - that is all.

Watch your thoughts if you wish …
you have seen most of them before.

Unless you are caught in this dream of time and space –
nothing is happening.

Resting as who you really are requires no effort or
movement.

Underneath the restless waves of the mind is found the
deep stillness of our natural state.
In dropping unnecessary mental activity, the natural
state can arise.

Look inwards – peace can be found there, waiting
calmly for you to find your way home.

Simply drop the stories created by thought.

Can you observe your thoughts without believing them?
Seeing them as simple ripples in consciousness …
sometimes useful - often useless.

Most thoughts serve to perpetuate the sense of a
separate self … the story of 'me'.
This is the default mode of our mind: designed to serve
and preserve our ego.

Dropping our interest in thoughts allows the possibility
of unchanging happiness arising.

Your mind may be totally chaotic,
with thoughts flying around randomly.
Let it be as it is – you are not that mind or those
thoughts.
You are what is watching them.

Leave thoughts alone … but don't turn this into
something else to do!

You can't achieve emptiness - you are emptiness.

You are that which watches
the witnessing of experience.
Do not become a watcher or witness –
just be that which sees the watching.

Consciousness arises from Awareness –
appears to itself as consciousness –
and merges back into Awareness.
It was never anything else but Awareness in disguise.

Thoughts make apparently real
what is essentially unreal.

Without your mind the world cannot exist;
so the world can be nothing except the product of mind.
You think it into existence.

Mind and world appear and pass away in manifestation;
all within unchanging Reality.
You are that Reality.

Be still – there is only you … creating and destroying
by the movement of mind.
You remain … unmoving and beyond concepts.
Nowhere to go … nothing to do ... already Home.

There is nothing outside reality –
forget about anything outside your Self
– you contain Universes!

Simply relax into your Self …
until the idea of anyone relaxing just drops away.

If there is only Oneness …
who is there to make the journey to enlightenment?
Duality is just another false concept.

Nothing is happening.
Happenings require time to be observed,
and time is not real.
There is just This … see?

A wave rises and falls as part of the ocean.
So does consciousness as part of Awareness.

Duality is necessary for dealing with the world.
Leave non-duality for making sense of Being.

Phenomenal truth is intellectualised;
Noumenal truth is lived.

Nothing is gained by self-realisation;
It is a matter of losing ignorance.

The game that consciousness plays with itself …
pretending to hide and forget where and what it is …
can be a spectator sport –
with only one ultimate winner: our Self.

What appears to change is the
manifestation of consciousness …
ripples on the surface of unchanging Awareness.

The world, body, mind and senses –
all require the movement of thought to exist.

The world is as real as you take yourself to be.

If you believe you exist as a separate entity,
the world appears as your prison;
and you are your own guard.

The thought that you are real is the primary delusion;
a false belief lacking any evidential basis.

Memory is simply time-creating thought.
A distortion of consciousness,
and a trick of the mind.

Are your night-time dreams any different from your
day-time experiences?
They are both the same – unreal!

The world can only exist due to the activity of the mind.
Thought has given permission for the world to appear.

As appearances in consciousness –
nothing really happens in either the waking or dreaming
states.

What you are is outside all appearances.
What you are cannot be known;
does not change,
and is in no way an object.

We might imagine that we are on a journey,
having a past and a future.
We are not going somewhere …
What we are has already arrived!

Whatever can be objectified or conceptualised,
you cannot be that.
If you can experience something,
you cannot be that something.
That applies to the most abstract concepts,
such as 'beingness' or 'presence'.

The ego dreads its own death …
but where is it when attention is elsewhere?
The ego is simply an illusion within a dream.

Thoughts arrive and pass away …
all equally irrelevant.
A thought about death is just that … a thought.
What is there to die?

The story of 'you' is responsible for all your suffering.

Whatever you find in your spiritual searching
cannot be Real.
Reality cannot be found … It is.

How can you become what you already are?

Drop the false beliefs and mistaken ideas and
discover who you are.

The story of your life is just that …
it does not define you.

Can you listen and look without expecting a result?

What drags you back into the story of 'you'?
What is the attraction … the gain?
Study that … shrivel it with bare attention …
and then come home to Who you really are.

The mind will always be doing its thing;
but there's no need to be caught in its headlights.
Look deeper inside ...
seek for what never changes.

Thoughts don't belong to you; and you are not
responsible for them.
Don't allow thoughts to define who you are.

Claiming ownership of thoughts strengthens the
delusion that there is a person thinking.

Does there have to be an owner of thoughts?
Can't they simply arise without the need for someone to
think them?

From absolute stillness the ripple of thought
disturbs the silence of consciousness,
and then sinks back into oblivion.
'No-one' need be involved.

Identifying with thoughts sets the scene for suffering.

The perfume of the Truth infuses all that is happening;
there is nothing more to understand ...
simply enjoy the fragrance.

The mind has produced the picture of your world.
Every opinion, idea and image
is the product of thought ...
you don't need to believe any of them.

Whatever forms you have named are in essence
formless and nameless.

Noumenally, all phenomenal objects cease to exist.

Using all your senses creates the world which is
transient and ephemeral.

See it as a story and don't be drawn into this imaginary
drama.

We are Spirit, with the option of
having a human experience.
Most of us take the option.
That's not a problem … experience the world,
enjoy what it offers …
but rest your attention within …
on what is unchanging.

Enjoy the road to enlightenment …
because when you wake up,
there won't be a road or any 'you' to enjoy it!

Perceiving differences creates all problems.
There is no difference between worldly
and spiritual ways of living.
Why imagine differences when there are none?

All actions arise spontaneously - there is no actor.

74

Be aware without concepts, interpretations or
conclusions.
Pure perception creates no choices.

Life is living the character called 'you'.
'You' have no free will and no destiny.
Give up any sense of control and enjoy the ride!

This ... everything you perceive now ...
has to be exactly how it is unfolding.
If one atom is out of place all this would cease to exist.

Everything ... This ... is just how it must be.

You imagine you are just a small part
of this incredible show.
Yet you are all of it!

You have never owned anything ...
not even your own life!

The heart is beating –
The lungs are breathing –
Let them have their play!

You are here to learn, to search, and to discover that you were always complete, and already home. You were dreaming of separation … but now wake up to Oneness.

Pure observing needs no observer.
Meditation requires no meditator.
Drop the concepts,
and just rest in I AM.

How do you gain the ultimate goal?
Stop … look … you are here!
What else could there be?
Any answer you come up with is just mind-stuff.

Can you drop the 'I' story?
Look underneath it to find who you truly are.
It's so simple.

Drop all desires for things to be different.
These desires are simply feeding the ego ...
and a strong ego is the cause of all suffering.

Freedom from desire is liberation from the 'I' story.

Feeling sad? Hopeless? Lost? Have another look!

If you mind what happens, contentment is lost.
Stop minding anything ... and peace arrives.

Things are just how they need to be ... relax and smile!

Whether you believe it or not ... all is well - always.

'You' don't have thoughts.
Thoughts arise and disappear in consciousness,
that's all.
It is believing that they are 'your' thoughts
that creates suffering.

When the 'I' disappears, nobody's there to celebrate.

We grasp at experiences and search for labels;
but in truth there are no such things.

There is a sense of being aliveness …
a feeling of existence.
Full stop.
The mind ignores the punctuation
and fills the silence with imagined
concepts and theories.
How silly!

Can we just say … in all humility … "I don't know"?

At heart, you are emptiness.
Not the body … not the mind.
Let them do what they will;
they won't last, and they
can't touch Who you are.

Progress is letting go … not accumulating.
We progressively uncover the unborn, formless Self
By stripping away everything that is not real:
images, concepts, beliefs,
all phenomena … all objects.
What is left?
Just this ….
and that's all we ever need, and Are!

Non-duality is just another dirty concept.
Flush it down the toilet!

Even 'nothingness' is an object in consciousness.

Let there be no ripples on the lake of awareness.

Whether you understand this or not,
You are always Home....
Welcome home!

Sneezing, belching, coughing, farting ...
All are welcome in the Great Perfection!

When the mind moves, thoughts are created;
be still then, and discover true peace.

Does a wave think it is dying,
as it slips gently back into the ocean?

Resisting what is = opening the door to misery.

Accepting what is = the road to wisdom.

"We are not responsible for our actions".

What a shocking, unacceptable statement.

Yet it is true.

Look at the situation logically ....
Thoughts appear... actions happen ...
Where is the thinker or the actor?
Show me where the 'person' lives!
It is not possible, because the 'person' is just a
collection of thoughts.
All that is here is energy moving through form.
Energy as actions, thoughts, perceptions, feelings.
Energy as consciousness appearing to itself.

You can call this energy God if you wish; I avoid this
as the word God is too loaded with delusional ideas
... a heavily contaminated concept. Whatever we call
'this', it is not an object; is not situated within time
or space, and has no characteristics. 'It' is everything
and nothing, and within it 'our' lives appear to exist.
I say 'appear to exist' because without conscious
awareness, we (and the universe) cease to be. All
appears as a consequence of consciousness, and is a
manifestation of consciousness. We are ripples on
the surface of conscious energy ... nothing more.
Ripples arise and subside, conditioned through
interdependent origination, and then settle back
into the silent, still ocean of being.

We are nothing more than psychosomatic apparatuses, conditioned by the environment and programmed by our DNA. There is no question of personal volition, choice or free will. There is no-one to possess these things. All that happens has to happen ... it is the spontaneous unfolding of life. We don't make decisions ... thoughts arise as they must. We don't act ... actions occur as they must, driven by universal forces and the smallest sub-atomic particles. Consciousness/God doesn't make mistakes, therefore this illusory self we call 'me' has never done anything and can therefore not be held responsible for any presumed action. There is no need for guilt or remorse, nor for fear and hope. Everything happened just as it had to; and had nothing to do with the imaginary 'you. Similarly, everything that will apparently happen will be inevitable and spontaneous, and will not be the result of any decision 'you' make. Actually in reality, no 'thing' ever happened, nor will any 'thing' ever happen.

This position is untenable for most people; and they are likely to react with anger and indignation. The concept of free will is precious to the ego, and underpins its claims to existence. Why should we continue to believe in an illusory 'self', in the absence of any credible evidence? You argue that you can decide to raise your right hand ... go on then

... do it! How do you know that was not a pre-determined action, over which you had no control?

That thought was pre-determined too, a programmed response to this challenge.
Nevertheless, 'you' claim ownership and responsibility for these actions and thoughts. Do you know what your next thoughts are going to be? .... of course not ... because they are not yours!   It is the false ego building its deceitful identity, assuming self-importance in the form of a lie. In reality, everything arises from the Nothingness which is a collection of possibilities of what might be.

You may now be feeling that if we are just puppets of a pre-determined fate, then why bother with planning or worrying about the future? Exactly!
Nevertheless, we are more than likely to continue with our mental habits and usual behaviour, as they are so deeply engrained.

The mind claims ownership and responsibility for too much. In its arrogance and self-importance it assumes that it can control what we do, and the consequences of our actions. This assumption does not stand up to critical investigation.
We have not a clue as to what will happen in the next moment. This breath or heart beat might be this body's last. Indeed, to claim ownership of the breath or heartbeat as 'mine' is another foolish

fantasy. Breathing, heartbeats, sensing, thinking ... all these things are happening spontaneously. Attaching meaning to them and attributing their cause to a 'person' is pure fiction.

Let go of these delusions, and peace arises. Stuff still happens ... the body grows old, becomes ill; the boiler breaks down; the roof needs mending; the car is stolen... all these events will continue. Your responses to all these situations determine the extent to which you will suffer. Resist – and you pay a price. Accept – and you reap the reward.

We are waves

Searching for the ocean ...

DUH!

The thought that arrives in your conscious awareness – is it yours? Did you choose to think it? Didn't it just appear? The thought 'I shall make a cup of tea' … did that just arrive and lead to action? A physical sensation leads to an associated thought: 'I need to visit the toilet'. All our actions are based on thoughts, and responses to thoughts … isn't this the truth? Please look for yourself.

If this is accepted, then the logical conclusion is that there are thoughts and actions, but no thinker and no actor. If you disagree, then show me the thinker/actor! If that's who you think you are – prove it! Where are you? Who are you?

Stepping back – as a painter might from a painting –
one can see more.
Releasing the concern with close control, perspective is
regained.

Things fall into place, and the interconnectedness of
everything is clearly recognised.

Actions are not seen as separate,
nor are decisions regarded as autonomous,
but all is perceived as one movement of energy.

There is no need for personal volition or motivation,
as these are illusory.
Stepping back and letting go of imaginary control is the
answer.

Fighting against the current of Life is foolish.
Instead, become Life and join the ecstasy of this
universal whirlpool!

———————————

If this is all there is …

Who needs hope?

This is how things are …

How could they be different?

Why should they be different?

It's only the mind which wants more …

More security –

More happiness –

More 'stuff' –

Splitting reality into good and bad;

Wanted and unwanted;

Past and future;

Self and other.

Can the mind fall silent?

Pause its game of division and judging?

Can the magic oneness of just this …

Whatever thoughts and sensations are here …

Be allowed, accepted and loved?

The only thing standing in the way of Understanding is belief.
Drop all beliefs ... they are distractions from What Is, and What Is does not need any faith.
It declares Itself without any room for doubt.
All things appear in their full perfection...
and on looking closer disappear ... into Oneness!

We are all expressions of Life Itself – why feel separate - or behave as if we were independent entities?
This enormous mistake was indeed the Fall from Grace, and is being repeated with each new human manifestation.

We are not in time, because we can observe it.
If we were in time, we would not be aware of movement or change.
Therefore we can step back and witness relative reality – this mind-generated show that appears so plausible.
Once established as a witness, we can let go of that concept as well, and simply BE.

There is only This ..
and if you don't like it,
blame the person you think you are ...
who doesn't exist ...
and then have a good laugh!

———

When there is no actor
all actions are just so ...
what else could they be?
Without anyone claiming ownership ...
all appearances are perfect.

———

Before thinking ...
Before the concepts and opinions ...
Before all 'things'.
There is Awareness.
This is what we are in reality.
There is nothing other than This.
Rest there.

———

The mind settles,
thoughts become quieter;
there is a pause in the day's restless activity.
Words cannot capture this ...
a sense of complete ease;
without judgement or description.

It's just This ...
warmth, sunlight,
birdsong, shifting sensations
playing a symphony of life.
There is no need for
purpose or meaning.

The chattering ego falls silent ...
and no words arise to
attempt definition or explanation.
This moving pen falters ... stops ...
nothing more is required.

What is there to teach?
… and who is there to teach it?

The presumption that one dream-figure
can show the way out of the dream
is laughable!
There may be waking within/to the dream …
or there may not. Period.

There is nothing to be done to hasten or
promote this 'awakening' …
as there is no-one to do anything.

What happens simply happens …
causelessly, spontaneously …
perfectly!

So make another cup of tea …
go for a walk …
pretend you are doing these things …
or take a step back and
enjoy watching Life unfold.

We are nothing but whirlpools
in the river of Life.
Appearing ...
creating a disturbance,
and disappearing again
into the flow of the Universe.
Nothing separate –
Nothing special.

———◦———

Could it be that this moment is
the most perfect moment in my life?
Or this moment? ... or this?
Are not all moments just perfect
the way they are?
Before thought ... this amazing dance
of sub-atomic 'wavicles'
(just pure energy)
produces this magnificent show.
How breath-taking!

But then thought intrudes with its
"yes, buts"; its defining and judging.
Stop! Drop all ideas and concepts.
Soak up this scene ... these sensations.
Drink in and celebrate the
wonder of this moment.

———◦———

Words, words … and more words!
How tired I am of them all.
They refer to all types of phenomena
… none of which exist.

Thoughts, too, are not real …
and yet dominate this waking dream.

Past, present, and future – wrapped up
in neat parcels of thoughts and words;
all illusory, yet insinuating
themselves into every experience.

Dulling our perception and
distorting our understanding;
we struggle for the simple
clarity of innocence.

Dropping false meanings and
crude interpretation,
for the purity of Being we leave
the words and surrender
to the beauty of silence.

You are not your face in the mirror –
you are what is looking.
The One that is the
origin of the Universe.

You are the single eye that
takes in everything,
and changes nothing.
Capacity for Life as it unfolds ... just as it is.

Forget everything you have been told;
drop all theories and beliefs;
just rest in the Awareness
that is your true face.

Read as much as you wish ...
strip the bookshops and libraries,
but use the information to deconstruct
rather than construct new concepts.

Liberate yourself through unlearning;
and let the Truth shine through,
burning away the mists of ego and delusion,
revealing nothing and everything!

Let my last word,
as the breath leaves my body,
be a whispered:
"YES!"

———◦———

Watching from a quiet height,
the performance continues,
... and the story unfolds.

———◦———

If you wish to know
who you really are –
Forget everything you think you know,
.... and just be present.

———◦———

Our life consists of seeing, hearing, tasting,
smelling, touching and thinking.
All these arise in Consciousness.
Without Consciousness nothing exists.
Consciousness is a disturbance of the silent
stillness of Awareness.
Our lives are thus simple disturbances of the
Absolute.

———◦———

Young seagull
whining for food –
parents fly away.

———————

The purpose of our lives
is to experience Joy –
and that includes loss,
suffering and misery.

Joy that is Real
contains all experience;
it is the mind that discriminates
and labels 'good' or 'bad'.

Going beyond judging,
all differences disappear –
there is simply Life
offering us opportunities to be present.

Before reaction, there is simply experiencing –
sensation and thoughts –
moments of pure perception
exploding with the joy of Being.

Be in those moments …

Feast on them ...
Live your heart out!

———

What now? ....
Something will happen –
the semblance of a decision –
and action may result.

But no-one decides ...
things just happen...
spontaneously, impersonally,
just the way they need to.

Sit back and watch the show ...
everything teaches us something ...
and stop pretending you have any control.

Cultivate equanimity.
Let go ... and enjoy the journey!

———

Child crying
Such noisy misery
Just for now.

... there's a getting up each morning;

doing stuff during the day;

and going to bed in the evening.

Things get done, but without any sense of 'doer-ship'.

Getting it

The whole idea of getting somewhere, or achieving some special state, is a big mistake. We are all already home, and just have to realise This is it! .... an aching back; the smell of fresh coffee, birds singing; every amazing perception as it unfolds here ... in this moment ...and the next.

The mind is a thought-generating machine without an 'off' switch ... there's no such thing as a quiet mind. There can be a mind that is useful; planning and deciding when needed. The mind that wanders aimlessly off into the past or future is a waste of energy, and so need not be paid any attention. Awareness needs no effort ... it's whatever is appearing now, and 'we' (awareness) can just be present and watch the show. Very simple, but not easy.

Questions starting with 'how?' imply that there's a method or path to follow; promising results at some future point. The future is just a concept. There is just this ... now! Let's be clear - there are no enlightened persons. There's no-one to become enlightened because there are no individuals. There are no real objects/things ... only perceptions and concepts appearing and disappearing in awareness. The false identification with mind and body is the fundamental error that 'apparent' humans suffer from, and the seeing through is done by no-one. Waking up to the dream can happen at any time, to 'anyone', causelessly. Oneness wants to win when it plays hide-and-seek with Itself; so sit back and enjoy the game! No doer, no separation, no sweat!

**The garden –
so many tasks …
tomorrow is OK.**

We are all driver-less cars
being driven through the
journeys of our lives.

Can we sit back and enjoy the views ....
and not be obsessed
with the illusion of control?

Release your grip on the steering wheel ...
take your feet off the pedals ...
Let go! and you will still arrive safely

———————

Fly on my knee
wringing its hands
what could possibly be wrong?

———————

You have built a prison of concepts ...
but look –
the door is open!

———————

100

Autumn leaves
chasing each other across the park –
and in the heart of all the movement;
perfect peace.

Nothing is happening
on the screen of Awareness;
but the Lord of the Dance
provides the entertainment.

For pity's sake – don't take this
dream of your life seriously!
Act your role playfully ...
and dance your heart out!

And at the end, you will know
that you played your part well;
laughed and cried in the right places,
and left the stage
having discovered that You
are the Eternal Playwright.

———

Raindrops falling –
coming home
to the Ocean.

———

There is nothing incomplete ...
it is all here;
everything in its place;
a perfect expression of the Divine.

Why then do we feel
something is missing –
that things should
somehow be different?

How could they possibly
be other than they are?
All is present as it should be ...
how else could it be?

Hush now – be quiet.
Let reality settle and calm the mind.
All is well ... better than well.
It is How It Is –
Right Now – Right Here
Shut up and enjoy it!

———————

If the dust of thought
obscures your understanding,
may these words act
as a vacuum cleaner!

———————

Do you mind?
In other words: do you want
anything in your life to be different?
Do you want what you don't have?
Do you have what you don't want?
If this is your experience,
then you are suffering.

Desire and aversion = suffering. Simple.
Not minding = freedom from suffering. Full stop.

So why do we suffer?
Because 'we' have been conditioned and
programmed
to think that we are the centre of 'our' universe;
and that what we want really matters.
It does not matter – get over it!
See the complete perfection of What Is …
and end suffering Now.

―――――◦―――――

When you board a train or plane
don't you place your baggage in the rack or locker?
Why would you continue to carry it?
So in life why not put down your baggage …
the weight of the past;
and rest while you enjoy the journey?

―――――◦―――――

103

The ring is made of gold
but the gold is not made of ring.
The ring needs the gold
in order to exist;
The gold needs nothing
in order to exist.

Awareness does not need any appearance or object;
but appearances and 'objects' require Awareness;
and are forms within Awareness...
simply expressions of Oneness.

———◦———

The autumn rain,
playing pianissimo on the roof,
doesn't disturb my reading.

———◦———

You are not the experience –
experiences occur within
the Awareness that you are.

Thus, you do not hear…
hearing happens.
You do not see …
seeing happens.
You do not think …
thinking happens …
not to any person, but to conscious Awareness.

No ownership … no responsibility!
You are freedom itself …
so release yourself from the burden of 'doership'.

It's a false assumption
that little you is causing or doing anything.
Let go - join the stream of Life
as it flows perfectly through the dream;
whilst, in actuality …
Nothing is happening!

Stop doing...
and let Being take over.
Being is already all there is ...
and it's just perfect.
Smile and rest ...
or struggle with your story of becoming;
the choice is there ...
with no-one to take it.
The story of 'I' will continue,
until it is seen as a story
(by no-one) and then enjoyed!

There are many paths
up the mountain –
but the view from the top
is the same for all.

Open the heart to this moment …
feel the simple miracle of Being here.
How amazing it is that you exist …
that you have happened!
And not just the fact that
you have occurred …
but that the whole universe
is appearing in the Awareness
that You are.

Everything has turned up
for your entertainment …
sky, clouds, birds,
breeze, trees, sunshine.
All this … just for You!

So don't moan about immigration,
or taxes, or the price of petrol …
Stop … look … be grateful.

Waking this morning,
and consciousness streamed in,
bringing sensations,
thoughts and moods;
a mixture of being.

Moment by moment,
all changes –
there is no safe port
in which to shelter …
Life will have its Way.

Behind, beyond it all,
but silently witnessing …
Awareness rests in its secret joy;
holding All.

I would rest there too,
but this organism drags me
on to complete its story.
Pausing to look, inquiry shows
that these actions, emotions, efforts,
are all That too … no separation!

Everything we need is just Here –
Right now.
Complete.
Perfect.
But we look for more,
Better,
Happier.

Wasting our time,
we overlook the simple
miracle of Being.

Life is unfolding in appearances,
unpredictably …
a triumph here…
a disaster there ..
a convincing and plausible melodrama.

Look behind the screen …
no-one is pulling the strings.
The dance reels across apparent lives,
creating and destroying in Its ecstasy.

And still we don't look
in the right direction.
Driven by fear, ambition,

greed and delusion…
division prospers, conflict spreads,
and separation and judgment
are all that can be seen.

Let us stop … be still …
Listen to the song that is
quietly humming in our hearts.
The song of Oneness …
inviting us home
to who we really are.
Here is Love …
the love we were always seeking
in the wrong places …
not knowing that our true nature
was Love … hiding from Itself.

In stillness let me breathe,
in silence let me sit,
in solitude let me live …
and in Love let me die.

Holding beliefs is like

eating cardboard....

they may fill you up,

but there's precious little nourishment.

Looking within,
there's space for everything,
and no need for anyone
to hold it all.

Autumn –
red leaves are jewels
decorating the lawn.

Waiting for words to arrive ...
they will come
when I get out of their way.

The physicists' point of singularity
is where nothing
expands into infinity.

What is it that watches change ...
that notices impermanence?
Go there.

We can never know God ...
but we can be God.

We suffer from a chronic delusional state
and a severe case of mistaken identity.
The cure is right here ...
under our noses...
before thought ...
let go into the Truth of who we really are.

And what can we ever find
but THIS …
from moment to moment
to every infinite moment.

All that we ever need
but appear to ignore …
this treasure trove of NOW.

The energy that we are
appears as body/mind…
temporarily forgetting its true identity.

Energy creates and destroys
in the relative world …
but essentially nothing changes.

The eternal and cosmic dance
whirls all into existence
and back to oblivion.

Beyond this marvellous chaos
the still, silent Source
Wears a secret smile.

Robin seeking shelter ...
winter winds arriving ...
may you be safe!

Dead leaves on the lawn
How precious...
Winter sunshine!

There are advantages to slowing down...
the senses are noticed more,
the warmth of sunshine on one's skin,
the support of a cushion in one's back ...
just so!
The taste of tea and smell of chocolate.
The sound of a familiar symphony,
freshly performed.
The greenness of a nettle leaf.
The nagging persistence and judgment
of the mind ... critical of doing nothing.
Why listen to such a work ethic
when fifty years of employment
have brought me the chance
to sit and watch seagulls?
Soon it may be time for some lunch ...
but that too can wait!

That I am, there is no doubt;
but **what** I am, there is no clue.
There is absolute confidence that
Awareness exists ... but it cannot be
located, described or measured.

When the character Graham is searched for,
all that is found is a pile of thoughts,
memories, opinions, preferences ...
bundled up into a story of a person.
There appears to be nobody at home.

... and yet, this humming aliveness,
this sense of simply being,
is immediate and inescapable
... and this is enough
... more than enough
... it is perfection.

Winter sky darkening ...
Pen poised for the next words to appear ...
The heart's song cannot be written.

Perhaps God has forgotten that
she was pretending to be everyone?
Who's going to remind her?
(let's realise that we are God in disguise ... job
done!)

The wise
realise
their disguise
... nothing more is needed.

We are all singing our song of Life ...
sight-reading the score ...
stumbling and mumbling in places;
unique and amazing performances ...
but who's listening?

Awareness has no need of a mind to know Itself.
Does the sun need a mirror to reflect its light?
The Light of Awareness is self-shining ...
and self-knowing.

Outside of time ... I AM ...
though good days and bad days seem to happen...
and change is all around;
hemming in with expectations, hopes and fears.
Awareness remains, watching, untouched,
still, silent and unchanging.
Dropping identity, there is a coming home to
Who I really am.

Tap into Love from its Source ...
the supply is endless.
Use love as something the ego creates
and you will quickly run dry.
Your true nature is infinite Love,
Joy and Happiness...
why ignore it and use a poor substitute?

No effort is required ...
all is free and is your birthright.
So drop the incessant demands
of the little self ...
and receive the blessings and wisdom
that were always yours –
always waiting for you to wake up.

Sitting on my shoulder is an enormous window
without edges … and spotless …
it contains everything …
and the world is welcomed in.

Suddenly all things that were outside
are now inside,
and I have made way for them.
In fact, I have become them.

No more separation between me
and other … subject and object.
Oneness has recognised Itself …
and there is a smile on my shoulders!

The Soul joins the Spirit dancing,
and the two become One.

Winter daydreams…
watery sunshine made warm
by conservatory glass.
What a gift!

Seagulls' cries … or are they?
Why label sounds?
There is simply hearing …
nothing heard … and no hearer.

Breathing … no-one doing that.
Heart beating; stomach digesting …
all happening independently.

Thinking happening … no thinker can be found.
Sensations being sensed … by no-one.

Words appearing …. no writer.
Just this miraculous unfolding of
Life and Love.

I may not have the right words
to lead you to the door of your Self.
The pointing to truth may not mean
enough,
or arouse the desire to move towards it.
The seeker may be too attached to the
seeking;
the ego too desperate to defy its death.

But perhaps a chink in the armour
of the little self will be revealed.
The light of seeing will squeeze
into the darkness of ignorance.

Questions may be asked that are
unanswerable
... and nothing will be quite the same again.

Was it decision or destiny
to put pen to paper just now?
Free will or determinism?
Whatever the answer, words arrive,
spilling across the page like this ....
Meaning? That too is indeterminate;
the interpretation lies with the reader.

Life is living Itself ... expressed
through the medium of this body-mind.
There may be no meaning –
a mind is needed to make sense of words.
All words are of the past ...
and thus all meaning arises, already dead.

Dropping the intellectual machinery
of interpretation and analysis ..
the scribbles become just ... LOVE.

Consciousness is all there is …
is there any more to say?
If that is the case, nothing arises
that is not an expression of Consciousness.

We can substitute Awareness
and quibble over semantics.
We can struggle to understand the
immense implications of such statements …
giving the mind a hernia from its exertions.

Or we can give up the effort
to comprehend Consciousness
… and be quiet.
Just sit … observe …
be puzzled, frightened, exasperated ...
it doesn't matter.
The dance of Life will continue
carrying us all in its arms
… and the music never ends.

Wanting more seems natural …
wanting less sounds strange.
Yet happiness is found in simple things …
you can list them yourself.
So whenever you ask where
the secret of happiness may be found ...
remember the answer …
simplify … simplify … SIMPLIFY!

Stay still ...

Be quiet …

Surrender to what is …

Let go ...   and let God!

What is the mind for?
Is it to make sense of
all the stuff that appears
in the awareness that we are?

Knowing simply sees this ...
there's no need to analyse or label
any of the intellect's activity.

Before perception, consciousness rests ...
ready to receive any and all
impressions that may arise.

The movie of life appears
on the screen of awareness ...
the screen we all share ...
the ground of our Being.

Allow every apparent thing to be there;
welcomed in silent knowing ..
and enjoy the show.
No-one's there to do anything else!

21ˢᵗ December

The shortest day of the year …
contracting into darkness …
as if holding its breath
before the exhalation of Spring.

Wind and rain sweep in from the West,
soaking the garden yet again,
and the bulbs beneath,
waiting to surprise us.

The puzzle of time invites us to
ponder the passing of the year …
another calendar of triumphs and misfortunes …
a new catalogue of memories to fill a diary.

Space and time seem to merge
into this experience ... here and now;
the passing show of sensation -
the miracle of just Being.

Can you stop rushing around
and take a moment to rest?
Taking a deeper breath … breathe out
slowly and notice a space between thoughts.

Right there … between thoughts …
in the heart of silence –
Is there any problem?
In fact, is there any thing?

Just an open awareness …
space for all things …
and no thing.
Rest there - you have come home.

Enjoy the game of being a person
Just don't take it personally!

Raindrops on the conservatory roof –
the staccato of a Bach partita –
such harmony!

Thought after thought … after thought… build up
the story of you.
Outside of thought is there a 'you' to be found?
Can you find any person that has not been created
by thought?
And without thought … just being …
resting in awareness - where are you?

This is nothing special – this is so ordinary
that seekers overlook the simplicity of Being.

You don't need another book, another teacher,
or another story of enlightenment.
Before thought – you ARE …
This is Love … already yours.

Playing the game of this human club,
I secretly cancel my subscription.

_____   _____

This 'me' that I think I am
seems nothing but a collection of mental habits;
some thoughts followed… others seen through.

A bunch of assumptions, based on
intellectual understanding of the Real.
Letting Life flow … but often giving it a sly push.

What's it all about?
… this game of mental trickery …
using the mind to work out that
the mind is useless.

Who is supposed to do anything?
… and why?
Any answer falls into duality's trap.

This pen is moving across the page,
apparently operated by the character 'graham'.
It will finish at the bottom of this page,
and then what?....
Life will answer … rest assured!

We spend our lives looking out at the world;
making sense of it all,
and making something of 'ourselves'.

We rarely get around to looking in to see
just who is looking out.
What is being aware?
What is making sense of it all?
... and who is making 'something' of who?

Assuming the brain is causing us
to be aware ...
and is the seat of consciousness ...
we don't question this empty guess.

Would we understand electricity
by dismantling our kitchen toaster?
What nonsense!

Could the brain be no more than
a processor of energy ...
a channelling of Life's appearances?

The mystery remains ...
Mind cannot comprehend its own origins.
So should we leave the question
unanswered
... and throw our apparent selves
into the beautiful and awful chaos
of the world?

Is there a world out there?
All that is experienced here
is a variety of sensations:
seeing, hearing, tasting,
smelling and touching...
and a stream of mental phenomena ...
thoughts, feeling and so on –
in an endless procession of
tedious intellectual activity.

Who is experiencing all this stuff?
Stop ... breathe ... listen ...
the silence will answer.

130

Looking out at a world full of things,
from this alive, spacious no-thing....
everything is allowed to be as it is.
The world is accepted into the Emptiness here –
nothing is left outside.

All the ugliness, trouble and misery
are invited to join the
beautiful, graceful and innocent,
in resting here.

The Centre is not touched (or touchable),
but embraces all things.
The openness contains all phenomena,
but is not any of these.

My true home is Here – not out there.
It is immortal and outside time …
and not finite and dying.
My Reality is not my appearance.

Mind creates the chasm.
Love is the bridge.
So what contracting thought divides
our open heart unites.

Let the words sink deeply
into the cognising intelligence
of your true nature.

Notice what is there before thought arises …
the awareness that is always there;
allowing and welcoming all experience.

Notice the noticing,
watch the awareness,
rest there –
it is Home.
May all beings come home to find peace.

January wind …
the jackdaws staying close
to the warm chimneys.

Who suffers? What is suffering?
Are thoughts and feelings not the cause of
our suffering?
And what are thoughts and feelings?
Are they the experiences that create our
lives?
Do they come and go?
Do they last?
Do they matter?
Do they make any permanent difference?
Are they true? Real?
Ask yourself these questions.

If these things come and go ...
and don't touch who you are ...
why do you then suffer?

Is it that you believe these ephemeral
appearances ...
these passing experiences?
Do they construct this fictional identity
that you imagine yourself to be?
Isn't it time you woke up to this dream?

As Consciousness we have no
characteristics or features ....
we contain them.

As the Source we have no
dimensions or locations ...
we embrace them.

As the Absolute we have no
history or destiny ...
we produce them.

As separate persons we have all of these ...
no wonder we suffer!

As the Ground of Being we need
none of these attributes ...
drop all claims to them.

As the phenomenal is absorbed
into the noumenal,
we realise our birthright, our true identity;
the self-shining Truth of who we really are.

Thoughts cannot be stopped ...
but they can be observed.

Imagine thoughts entering your house
through the front door ...
a continuous stream of visitors.

These unwanted and uninvited guests
clutter up every room ...
milling around in aimless circles.

There seems no escape from these impostors ...
but there is one.

Open the back door ... ignore the unwanted visitors ...
don't feed them with your attention.

They all find their way out eventually ...
leaving you in peace and quiet,
watching their entrances and exits
from the comfort of your sofa!

The brain is a radio receiver,
tuned to the 'blah – blah' station by default.
This can be changed ... the non-dual channel is
an alternative ...
where the message is simply awareness.
But what if the radio is switched off?
No reception ... no signal ...
but a background of Being ... without any
listener?

The dazzling darkness of the Absolute;
needing presence to recognise Itself....
Consciousness arises from such movement,
as ripples appearing across a silent lake.

Satchitananda

We are...
we know that we are ...
and we love being.
Simple?
Why complicate it with a story of a life?

Consciousness knows itself in the light of Awareness.
Without the movement of existence there is no thing ...
no light to see any object.

Each night we return to this nothingness ...
the bare Awareness that we truly are.
Waking begins the commotion of
mental activity we call life ...
the chattering of thoughts,
the symphony of sensations.
We can watch the show, or join the party.
Do we have a choice?
Who is there to choose?

The elements of our body/mind will exist for a while ...
in apparent time ...
a minute, month, year ... it matters not.
When these elements fall apart, Consciousness leaves,
and the energy that was set free,
falls ... settles ... and becomes still. Again.

There never was any person.
You are not a person.
I am not a person.
Get over it ... and wake up!

Repeat after me: "I am not a person".
You, the reader, are not a person.
You don't want to hear that, do you?
Be honest … it's the worst possible news, isn't it?

You don't have to believe me …
just look for yourself.
Exactly where are you?
In the head? … the body?
Consciousness? What is that?

Are you anything other than a bunch of
thoughts and memories thrown together
to create the story of a life?
… a collection of labels?

So what are you really?
Ssssshhhh … don't answer that!
Let the question sit there …
marinating … maturing…
(the answer is already there isn't it?)!